SHARING YOUR FAITH WITHOUT BEING PUSHY

T0040168

REAL
CONVERSATIONS

PARTICIPANT'S GUIDE
(includes Leader's Guide)

JONATHAN MCKEE

 **ZONDERVAN®**
.com

 youth
specialties

ZONDERVAN.com/
AUTHORTRACKER
follow your favorite authors

ZONDERVAN

Real Conversations Participant's Guide
Copyright © 2012 by Jonathan McKee

YS Youth Specialties is a trademark of YOUTHWORKS!, INCORPORATED and is registered with the United States Patent and Trademark Office.

Requests for information should be addressed to:
Zondervan, *Grand Rapids, Michigan* 49530

ISBN 978-0-310-89080-5

Cover design: Knail
Interior design: Ben Fetterley / Matthew Van Zomeren

Printed in the United States of America

12 13 14 15 16 17 18 /DCI/ 21 20 19 18 17 16 15 14 13 12 11 10 9 8 7 6 5 4 3 2 1

CONTENTS

CONTENTS

PARTICIPANT'S
GUIDE

Sharing my faith terrifies me.

Seriously. I can't explain why, but I'm always frightened when I get the opportunity to talk to others about my relationship with Jesus.

For some reason I have no problem standing onstage in front of a thousand students and talking about Jesus. That's not frightening to me at all.

But if you put me on a plane next to a guy and tell me to try to talk with him about Jesus . . . *I'm petrified!*

What do you say in this situation?

"Hey man, did you ever consider what would happen to your soul if this plane went down in flames? Because those flames are nothing like the flames of . . . HELL!"

Nope. Sorry. Can't do it.

I can't be that pushy guy who makes everybody feel awkward.

Funny thing . . . I never got the sense that Jesus did that, either.

Several years ago I brought some middle school kids to a fun event with hundreds of other teenagers. A powerful speaker preached the gospel that night, and a swarm of students came forward to make commitments to Christ. A couple of the kids I brought went forward, had a conversation with a counselor, and put their trust in Jesus.

But not Kelly.

I knew Kelly and her friends pretty well; I was just excited that they actually showed up. Kelly didn't really like to talk about God or Jesus, but she liked hanging out with her friends, even at an evangelistic event like this.

At the end of the evening we were all walking to our van. Two counselors from the event—older teenagers who had just prayed with some kids moments before—were walking out to their car, ecstatic that they had an opportunity to share the gospel that night. In their excitement they were boldly talking with groups of kids in the parking lot, asking questions and giving short soliloquies along the way.

The counselors eventually ended up in front of a handful of girls from our group.

One of those girls was Kelly.

"So . . . what did you think of tonight?" they asked Kelly.

"It was all right," she reluctantly answered, exchanging glances with her friends, wondering who these guys were.

"What did you think of the speaker?"

"He's cool."

"What did you think when he gave the opportunity for you to give your life to Jesus?"

Walking faster and trying to end the dialogue, Kelly responded, "I don't get into that serious stuff."

But these teenage guys wouldn't give up: "When will it be time for you to get serious?" they asked.

"I don't know," Kelly responded. "I just don't get into it." Kelly and the girls arrived at the van by now, opened the door and scurried inside.

But these two guys actually stood at the open door of the van and continued their onslaught of questions. "Well, what if time runs out? Like if you were to get into a car accident on the way home tonight? Would you wish you had gotten serious?"

Kelly was sitting against the far side of the van now, attempting to look out the window the other way. "I really don't want to talk about this serious stuff right now," she replied, trying to end the interrogation.

These two didn't know when to quit. By the time I arrived—unfortunately a few minutes behind my group—one of the guys was giving an elaborate illustration of how no one, regardless of how good a jumper they were, could jump across the great chasm that exists between us and God. Kelly and her friends looked like cats, cornered in an alley by a stray dog.

I started up the van and quickly announced it was time to go. The two fellows looked at me as if I were Satan incarnate and actually still tried to continue their sales pitch. I pressed the accelerator, and as we exited the parking lot I'll never forget what Kelly said:

"I'll never go to one of these events again!"

PUSHY OR SILENT

When Christians see an opportunity to share their faith, I find that they often do *too much* or *too little*. They're either too pushy . . . or the polar opposite—silent.

Neither extreme is good.

I've seen numerous Christians confuse "pushiness" with "boldness." Uh, newsflash: *Jesus wasn't pushy.*

Here are the facts:

- People always run away from pushy Christians constantly trying to give gospel sales pitches.
- People didn't run from Jesus. As a matter of fact, the more serious the sinner, the more Jesus was attractive—a draw.

If you read about Jesus in the Bible's Gospels (Matthew, Mark, Luke, and John), I believe you'll start to notice how much Jesus cared for the people he encountered, meeting their physical needs, feeding them, and even healing them. Jesus' compassion for the crowds opened doors to countless conversations.

But I guess some Christians missed those parts of the Bible, because often you'll see them using pushy methods: People holding signs that say *Repent and turn from your sins!* Or shouting into bullhorns on street corners. You'll even see people using the tactics those two teenage guys tried on Kelly.

When did Jesus do any of that?

Funny, if you ask these pushy Christians why they do these things, they'll often respond, "Because, of the hundreds of people we encounter, if just one person were to put faith in Jesus, then it would be worth it."

But what about the hundreds who were turned off or embittered or became resentful? How does that calculate into their little math equation?

How does Kelly factor in?

Perhaps we need to stop confusing pushiness with boldness. Maybe we need to stop scaring people away under the guise of evangelism.

Now hear this: Jesus wasn't *pushy*.

But he wasn't *silent*, either.

Sadly some Christians are so worried about being pushy that they opt for the polar opposite—they don't say a thing! Don't get me wrong: This "silent" group can be a kind and compassionate bunch. They're kind to their neighbors and feed the homeless.

They just never tell anyone *why* they do what they do.

Or they say, "Because Jesus fed people and healed people."

Really? That's all he did? What Bible are they reading?

I had heard this argument so frequently that I finally decided to do a study of the Gospels (I documented my findings in one of my previous books, CONNECT). I noted every instance when Jesus encountered another person. I marked a green dot in my Bible (yep, I just took a green marker and made a dot right on the pages in my Bible) whenever Jesus brought up God or the truth of the Scriptures, and I marked a red dot if he simply loved people with acts of compassion or service.

When I finished this study, it was clear that Jesus was *not* afraid to share the truth (a lot of green dots). There were times when he just met people's physical needs (some red dots), but most of the time he "brought it up" (a lot more green than red dots). Sometimes he preached, sometimes he fed or healed people, and sometimes he did both.

I believe many Christians forget this balance. The more that "pushy" Christians read the gospel with open eyes, the more they would see how much Jesus cared for people as a whole—feeding them and healing them. At the same time, the more that "silent" Christians read the Gospels with hearing ears, the more they would notice how often Jesus was unafraid to enter into conversations about the hard truth.

Jesus wasn't *pushy* or *silent*.

As we dive into this training, I believe we'll find that sharing our faith with our friends might be frightening; it might even make us reevaluate how we're living our lives and how we treat others . . . but sharing our faith in Jesus will never require us to be pushy.

The fact is, when we live out our faith authentically, we'll begin to notice open doors for real conversations about our faith.

Maybe it's time for us to squash this myth of pushiness . . . and at the same time, break the silence with *real conversations* about an authentic faith.

OUR FAITH

AN AUTHENTIC FAITH OPENING DOORS TO REAL CONVERSATIONS

ALONE TIME

Grab a pen and read this section while you're alone.

SCARED SILENT

In this training we're tackling a scary subject for some of us: *Sharing our faith.* I'll be the first to admit it's scary for me. (If you haven't looked at the READ THIS FIRST section at the beginning of this book, quickly read it now—I believe you'll be relieved by what I have to say.)

Some of us might have some big fears when it comes to sharing our faith. Maybe we don't know what to say. Maybe we're afraid to bring it up because our friends have seen how imperfect we are. Sadly, sometimes these fears scare us silent.

That's why we're gonna look at these fears right now . . . and side-kick them in the face! (Sorry, sometimes I get a little bit expressive.)

This guide not only will help us sort through these fears and feelings, but also it will equip us to live out an authentic faith, which will open doors to authentic conversations.

I believe you'll really enjoy this!

WHAT ABOUT YOU?

Take a moment and write down your feelings about sharing your faith with others. I'll ask you a few candid questions, and you write down your answers. (This is just between you and God. No one else will see this.)

1. What's your biggest fear about sharing your faith with your friends?

2. What would make it easier for you to share your faith with your friends?

The Apostle Paul—after all of his religious rearing and training—knew he couldn't depend on his own wisdom and power to talk to others about God. He explained this in one of his letters to the church in Corinth:

> [1]And so it was with me, brothers and sisters. When I came to you, I did not come with eloquence or human wisdom as I proclaimed to you the testimony about God. [2]For I resolved to know nothing while I was with you except Jesus Christ and him crucified. [3]I came to you in weakness with great fear and trembling. [4]My message and my preaching were not with wise and persuasive words, but with a demonstration of the Spirit's power, [5]so that your faith might not rest on human wisdom, but on God's power. (1 Corinthians 2:1-5)

3. What are the some of the words Paul used in verse 3 to describe how he approached the people of Corinth?

4. What's the one thing Paul resolved to know, mentioned in verse 2?

5. What was the source of his power for his message and preaching, mentioned in verse 4?

As smart as Paul was, he knew he shouldn't get cocky and rely on his own abilities. Paul knew his wisdom and fancy words were nothing compared to God's power. So he decided to focus only on the message of Christ on the cross, giving Jesus all the attention and all the credit. Paul basically said, "It wasn't because of my good preaching and slick presentation that you guys were convinced; it was by God's power."

6. Why would it be smarter to rely on God rather than our own abilities?

7. What elements of human wisdom do you sometimes rely on?

8. What would be a way that you could rely on God's power instead of human wisdom?

In this section of Paul's letter to the Corinthians, he makes it clear that he didn't come to them with any eloquence or wisdom; instead he came in weakness and fear. This evident weakness made it clear to others that Paul was relying on God's power, not his own strength or street smarts! In other words, when people looked at Paul, they didn't see a really smart guy—they saw a guy whom God was working through. The focus was on God, not Paul.

9. What would this look like in your life? (pointing to God, not yourself)

A MOMENT TO PRAY

Let's talk to God about this.

Talking to God is simple. You don't need to use any magic words. In Matthew, chapter 6, Jesus told his disciples just to go into their rooms, close their doors, and be real with God who sees everything unseen (so we might as well be real with God—who knows everything about us anyway).

So let's do that now. Take a minute and pray specifically that we can rely on God's power instead of our own wisdom in the way we detailed in question #8. Let's also pray that we can live out an authentic faith that will point other people to God.

LARGE GROUP TIME

Do this section with your group: I find it helpful to talk with other Christians and discuss life and receive encouragement to live out my faith in Jesus. That's why we're going to do much of this training as a group.

OPTIONAL ICEBREAKER
Your leader will take us through a fun activity to break the ice during this large group time.

WATCH SECTION 1 OF DVD
A quick word from Jonathan: Hey! This is cool. You've been reading what I asked you to read! Now you get to hear what I have to say. Watch SECTION 1 of the DVD right now as we talk about how sharing our faith begins with . . . *our own faith!*

GROUP ACTIVITY
Your leader will take us through an activity to help us process what we just learned.

SMALL GROUP DISCUSSION QUESTIONS
Think About This: Many of us might get a little uncomfortable when we talk about sharing our faith. Maybe it's because we know that it has a lot to do with how we live out our own faith. Maybe it's because we're just scared of having conversations about our faith with our friends. Either way . . . you're not alone. Most of us probably feel scared and ill-equipped at times.

1. Some of us might have had some bad experiences or witnessed some really negative examples of people telling
   others about Jesus. Does anyone want to share one of those
   experiences?

2. Many of us have probably encountered people with very
   genuine faith in Jesus—so real that you almost wanted to ask
   them about it. Does someone want to share what you saw in
   this person that made you think, "I'd like a faith like that" or
   "If I had questions about my faith, I'd want to talk with her"?

3. Jonathan introduced the session talking about the feelings,
   fears, or apprehensions many of us might feel if we found out
   that tomorrow one of our friends was going to ask us about
   our faith. Let's look at our feelings honestly for a moment:
   How would you feel right now if you knew that tomorrow
   you'd have to share your faith with a friend? Why would you
   feel like that?

In the verses we just studied, we learned that sharing our faith requires WORDS and ACTION. First, we live out our faith in our ACTIONS. And then those actions—that authentic faith, the "hope" others see in our lives—open the doors to conversations: WORDS.

4. What does it look like to do what the verse says and "revere Christ as Lord"?

5. In what ways might your friends see that authentic faith and "hope" in you?

6. What areas in your life right now might distract people from seeing that "hope" in you?

7. What can do to try to fix those distractions and live a more authentic life?

8. Are you ready to have conversations, explaining the reason for your hope? What would you say?

SMALL GROUP WRAP-UP

Hopefully this training we're doing together will help us not only to live out that hope of Christ in our lives, but also to prepare us for those real conversations. As we continue this training, we'll talk a little bit more about how to articulate our faith.

SOMETHING YOU CAN DO THIS WEEK

We've just discussed the "hope" in our lives. This made us consider two areas:

1. Where friends see authentic faith and "hope" in our lives.
2. Areas where we're weak, and where our actions distract others from seeing the hope in our lives.

Let's start off each morning this week in prayer and pray about those two specific areas of our lives. Pray that God will help us, continue to work through us, and reveal himself to others through our actions. Also pray that God will help us get rid of the "sin that so easily entangles [us]." (Hebrews 12:1-2)

OUR MISSION
FIELD

THE PEOPLE YOU
ENCOUNTER DAY TO DAY

ALONE TIME

Grab a pen and read this section while you're alone.

THE PEOPLE YOU ENCOUNTER

In the last session we discussed how "sharing our faith" begins with our own faith. Hopefully for the last week you've been praying and asking God to help you live an authentic faith.

An authentic faith will open the door to real conversations with the people we encounter each day.

Today we're going to take a closer look at the types of people we will encounter.

WHAT ABOUT YOU?

Take a moment and think about two or three friends with whom you might want to share your faith. Ask yourself who you'd like to talk to if you knew that, for whatever reason, you and your friends would actually have a pleasant conversation about your faith. Write their names in the blanks provided.

Friends I want to reach out to:

_____

_____

_____

Over the next few weeks we'll specifically pray for these friends and ask God to reveal himself through us so we might have an opportunity to live out our faith and maybe even dialogue about it with our friends. Pray that our friends might be willing to listen and receive what we have to say, too.

In the book of Matthew, Jesus talks about how people receive our message. He cleverly tells it in the form of a parable.

[1] That same day Jesus went out of the house and sat by the lake.
[2] Such large crowds gathered around him that he got into a boat and sat in it, while all the people stood on the shore. [3] Then he told them many things in parables, saying: "A farmer went out to sow his seed. [4] As he was scattering the seed, some fell along the path, and the birds came and ate it up. [5] Some fell on rocky places, where it did not have much soil. It sprang up quickly, because the soil was shallow. [6] But when the sun came up, the plants were scorched, and they withered because they had no root. [7] Other seed fell among thorns, which grew up and choked the plants.
[8] Still other seed fell on good soil, where it produced a crop—a hundred, sixty or thirty times what was sown. (Matthew 13:1-8)

1. What do you suppose the seed represents?

2. What do you suppose the different soils represent?

Jesus goes on to explain the parable a few verses later:

[18] "Listen then to what the parable of the sower means: [19] When anyone hears the message about the kingdom and does not understand it, the evil one comes and snatches away what was sown in

their heart. This is the seed sown along the path. [20] The seed falling on rocky ground refers to someone who hears the word and at once receives it with joy. [21] But since they have no root, they last only a short time. When trouble or persecution comes because of the word, they quickly fall away. [22] The seed falling among the thorns refers to someone who hears the word, but the worries of this life and the deceitfulness of wealth choke the word, making it unfruitful. [23] But the seed falling on good soil refers to someone who hears the word and understands it. This is the one who produces a crop, yielding a hundred, sixty or thirty times what was sown." (Matthew 13:18-23)

Jesus explains that the sower shares "messages about the kingdom" (the seed). People (the soils) receive these seeds in different ways.

3. Describe a person who's like the path.

4. Describe a person who's like the rocky ground.

5. Describe a person who's like the thorns.

6. Describe a person who's like the good soil.

7. Which of these soils have you observed at your school and in
your group of friends?

I always find it interesting that, in this parable, the sower doesn't
sow different kinds of seeds. The seeds are all the *same message* about
the kingdom. The difference is in the *soil*—the person receiving the
message.

In other words, the people we encounter will always receive
God's message differently. This session will hopefully prepare us for
encountering these various people.

A MOMENT TO PRAY

Let's talk to God about this.

In the last session I mentioned that talking to God is simple. We
just want to get alone and get real with God just like Jesus told us in
Matthew, chapter 6.

Let's do that now. Take a minute and specifically pray for the
friends we just wrote about here, and ask God to reveal himself
through us so we might have opportunities to live out our faith and
maybe even dialogue about it with these friends.

LARGE GROUP TIME

Do this section with your group: Here's the section of this training that we'll do together with a group of believers.

OPTIONAL ICEBREAKER

Your leader will take us through a fun activity to break the ice during this large group time.

WATCH SECTION 2 OF DVD

A quick word from Jonathan: Now you get another chance to hear what I have to say. Watch SECTION 2 of the DVD right now as we talk about our mission field, the people we encounter day to day.

GROUP ACTIVITY

Your leader will take us through an activity to help us process what we just learned.

SMALL GROUP DISCUSSION QUESTIONS

Think About This: In the video we heard Jesus' commission to his followers, asking them (and us) to go and make disciples. Jonathan said this could be said like this: *"While you're at home, school, sports, and with friends . . . as you're doing life day to day . . . make a conscious effort to make disciples."*

1. Of those places (home, school, sports, hanging with friends after school), which makes it the most difficult to think

about this process of discipleship—reaching out to our friends and meeting their spiritual needs? Why is this difficult?

2. Which of the three types of OUTREACH kids is the hardest to reach? Why?

3. What do you suppose is the *worst* way to reach out to them?

4. What do you suppose is a *good* way to try to reach out to them?

5. Which of the three types of OUTREACH kids is the easiest to reach? Why?

6. How do you reach out to them?

SMALL GROUP WRAP-UP

I will hand each of you a 3x5 card and pen. I want you to think of someone you know who's an OUTREACH kid. Write his or her name on this card. Now I want you to think of some of the good ideas you've heard in our discussion and around this group today that might help you take the first steps toward reaching out to them. Write down one idea of something you can do this week.

Does anyone want to share your idea around the group?

Let's close and pray specifically for each of these kids we want to reach out to this week.

SOMETHING YOU CAN DO THIS WEEK

We've just taken a detailed look at our mission field—the people we encounter each day at home, school, sports, while hanging with friends . . . wherever! We realize these people may receive God's message differently from the way we receive it.

Let's start off each morning this week specifically praying for the people whose names we wrote down in the beginning of this session. Let's pray that we continue to live an authentic faith that might open the door to real conversations with these people.

OUR
APPROACH

WHEN ACTIONS OPEN
DOORS FOR WORDS

ALONE TIME

Grab a pen and read this section while you're alone.

TIMING IS EVERYTHING

In the last session we took a detailed look at our mission field—the people we encounter each day at home, school, sports, while hanging with friends . . . wherever! We also wrote down the names of three friends we want to reach out to with God's message of love and grace. Hopefully we've been praying about this for the last week.

Today we'll start thinking about how we approach conversations with these friends. After all, we don't want to be pushy—but at the same time we want to be bold and look for open doors to have real conversations.

Now let me tell you what we're *not* going to do. We won't memorize some sales pitch and randomly try to force it on people. This does more harm than good.

Think about it: Someone may know *how* to present the gospel message, all kinds of cool stories and illustrations, and even convincing methods of persuasion. But it doesn't matter how good the presentation is if the presenters don't have any sense of *when* to present it.

Over a decade of marriage to my wife, I've learned a lot about listening.

Unfortunately I've learned most of it the hard way. In our first year of marriage, Lori would come home from a hard day and share a problem she faced. I, being the man with all the answers, was gracious enough to solve those problems for her—explaining what she did wrong and what she needed to do in the future. After several experiences of sleeping on the couch I realized, "Hey . . . she doesn't want answers! She just wants someone to *listen* to her!"

Sometimes people just need someone to *listen*. Sometimes people just need a friend. Being a friend will open the door in God's timing. God will provide a number of opportunities for you to share your faith with your friends. Presenting the gospel is the easy part; the tough part is knowing *when* and finding those open doors.

So let's dive in and discuss our approach.

WHAT ABOUT YOU?

Take a moment and think about the names of the friends you wrote down in the last session.

1. Have you ever had an opportunity to share your faith with these friends or others in the past? How did you approach the subject?

2. Have you ever witnessed someone being too pushy while sharing about Jesus? What should that person have done differently?

Jesus constantly found himself in situations in which the subject of God, faith, or eternal life emerged. Jesus never seemed pushy, yet he brought up the subject quite frequently. One example is when he went into Samaria with his disciples. Most of the religious people tried to avoid Samaria—they didn't like the Samaritans at all. But Jesus saw this as an opportunity to talk with some people who were often ignored.

[4] Now he had to go through Samaria. [5] So he came to a town in Samaria called Sychar, near the plot of ground Jacob had given to his son Joseph. [6] Jacob's well was there, and Jesus, tired as he was from the journey, sat down by the well. It was about noon.

[7] When a Samaritan woman came to draw water, Jesus said to her, "Will you give me a drink?" [8] (His disciples had gone into the town to buy food.)

[9] The Samaritan woman said to him, "You are a Jew and I am a Samaritan woman. How can you ask me for a drink?" (For Jews do not associate with Samaritans.)

[10] Jesus answered her, "If you knew the gift of God and who it is that asks you for a drink, you would have asked him and he would have given you living water."

[11] "Sir," the woman said, "you have nothing to draw with and the well is deep. Where can you get this living water? [12] Are you greater than our father Jacob, who gave us the well and drank from it himself, as did also his sons and his livestock?"

[13] Jesus answered, "Everyone who drinks this water will be thirsty again, [14] but whoever drinks the water I give them will never thirst. Indeed, the water I give them will become in them a spring of water welling up to eternal life."

[15] The woman said to him, "Sir, give me this water so that I won't get thirsty and have to keep coming here to draw water." (John 4:4-15)

3. Most of the religious people of the day didn't associate with Samaritans. Why do you suppose Jesus decided to visit Samaria and start a conversation with this woman?

4. How do you suppose this woman felt when Jesus started talking with her?

5. Is there a place you could go to start conversations with people who're typically ignored or overlooked?

6. Jesus and the woman talked about water, and the next thing we know he was having a spiritual conversation with the woman! How did he do that?

7. Why do you suppose this woman was so interested in what Jesus had to say?

In this Bible passage, Jesus talks about "living water" and quenching thirst to get this woman's attention. As we read the entire passage, this woman wasn't only thirsty physically—she was thirsty *spiritually*. Many people we encounter might be thirsting for something to fill the emptiness in their lives. God frequently opens doors for us to offer hope to people in these otherwise hopeless situations.

A MOMENT TO PRAY

Let's talk to God about this.

In the last couple of sessions I mentioned that talking to God is simple. We just want to get alone and get real with God, just like Jesus told us in Matthew, chapter 6.

Let's do that now. Take a minute and specifically pray for opportunities to reach out to people who are often ignored or overlooked. Let's also pray for Spirit-led boldness to share the truth in these situations—but without being pushy.

LARGE GROUP TIME

Do this section with your group: Here's the section of this training that we'll do together with a group of believers.

OPTIONAL ICEBREAKER
Your leader will take us through a fun activity to break the ice during this large group time.

WATCH SECTION 3 OF DVD
A quick word from Jonathan: Now you get another chance to hear what I have to say. Watch SECTION 3 of the DVD right now as we talk about how we approach conversations with our friends. After all, we don't want to be pushy, but at the same time we want to be bold and look for open doors to have real conversations.

GROUP ACTIVITY
Your leader will take us through an activity to help us process what was just presented.

SMALL GROUP DISCUSSION QUESTIONS
Think About This: In the video Jonathan talks about two extreme examples of how we approach our friends—both of them lousy ways to share our faith.

1. What are the two negative examples Jonathan gives?

2. Which extreme approach do you tend to gravitate toward? Why?

3. What's something you could do to avoid floating toward that extreme?

4. Jonathan says there's another, more balanced approach. What does he call this approach? Why do you suppose he calls it that?

5. How can you be more Spirit-led?

In 1 Peter 5:5-7, the apostle writes:

All of you, clothe yourselves with humility toward one another,
because,
"God opposes the proud but shows favor to the humble."
6 Humble yourselves, therefore, under God's mighty hand, that
he may lift you up in due time. 7 Cast all your anxiety on him
because he cares for you.

In the video, Jonathan reminds us that throughout the Bible,
God frequently tells us to "humble ourselves." God doesn't want us
to make the mistake of trying to make it on our own; God wants us
to depend on him.

6. According to 1 Peter 5:6, what happens when we humble
   ourselves?

7. How can you humble yourself—in other words, what does
   this look like in your life?

8. How do you suppose God might lift you up?

If the idea of sharing your faith scares you, then simply humble yourself.

God actually *wants* you to give him your worry and anxiety about this. Because when you're humble enough to do that, God will take care of you.

9. God wants us to rely on him at all times. How is this truth especially helpful to us when we're trying to engage in real conversations about our faith with our friends?

SMALL GROUP WRAP-UP

This "Spirit-led" approach isn't pushy ... but it is bold.

As we live out our faith authentically, people will notice our actions. If we're humble enough to rely on God and let his Spirit give us boldness, God will open doors for real, honest conversations. They might start with us asking good questions and being ready to actually listen.

This whole process might seem scary at times. That's why it's reassuring to know that the Holy Spirit is right there with us, even giving us the right words to say.

I'm glad we're not in this alone!

SOMETHING YOU CAN DO THIS WEEK

The Spirit-led approach requires us to be good listeners—not just with our friends, but *with God's Spirit*. Sometimes the Holy Spirit might ask us to reach out to someone and care for that person. For example, maybe we'll see a homeless person who's asking for food; maybe we'll see a fellow student sitting alone on campus. God might prompt you to walk over and start a conversation with that person.

We must be ready to listen and respond when God prompts us to show compassion. We must be ready to *actually listen* to the person to whom we're reaching out.

Let's start each morning this week in prayer and pray the words that Jonathan encourages us to pray: "God, how can I represent you today in *word* and *action*?" Let's pray these words every morning and then keep our ears ready to listen throughout the day. In addition, let's remember to keep praying for the three friends whose names we wrote down last week. Let's ask God to specifically help us represent him in word and action to those friends.

OUR
MESSAGE

SHARING THE REASON FOR YOUR HOPE

ALONE TIME

Grab a pen and read this section while you're alone.

NOW WHAT?

For the last three weeks we've been discussing our faith, our mission field, and our approach. All of this has finally brought us to the point where we actually "talk" with our friends about our faith.

Now you might be wondering, "So what do I say?"

Think about this: Let's say you've already done everything we've been talking about so far:

> **OUR FAITH**—You live out an authentic faith, allowing God to slowly rid you of those sins that so easily entangle you.
>
> **OUR MISSION FIELD**—You think about the people you want to reach and pray for them daily.
>
> **OUR APPROACH**—You look for opportunities to reach out to these people in word and action, listening to the Holy Spirit and paying attention to the Spirit's "nudges."

Now what?

Perhaps one of the friends you've been praying for opens up to you and gets real about his search for meaning in his life. You listen carefully to your friend, and the Holy Spirit "nudges" you to share your faith . . .

At this point, what do you say?

WHAT ABOUT YOU?

If you live out an authentic faith, the Holy Spirit will open doors to real conversations in which you have opportunities to share the reason for the hope that lives inside you. The question is, *What do you share?*

1. Have you ever had the opportunity to share your faith? If so, what happened?

2. Do you believe you explained your faith well enough? Why or why not?

3. What essentials do you believe people need to know about a relationship with God?

The more you read the Bible, the more you'll learn about what our relationship with God is all about. From the very beginning—in the book of Genesis—all the way until the time of Jesus, you'll see the same elements again and again: *God's love for us* coupled with *our decisions to trust in God . . . or not.*

That pretty much sums it up.

Over and over again, God loved people and communicated his desire to have a relationship with them. And people either trusted God or decided to do things their own way.

In the last few sessions we've been discussing what "trusting" God looks like in our own lives. An authentic faith doesn't mean we're perfect. But when we trust in Jesus, putting his words into practice, we begin to live more like him.

And don't underestimate the extent to which people around us notice this kind of authentic faith. Our friends are probably good at spotting "fake."

Young people today are pretty skeptical of religion in general. That's where true Christianity stands out from most "religion." Our relationship with God is based on faith, not how "good" we are (or aren't). As we share our faith with our friends, we should be sure to communicate this simple, biblical truth. We can't earn our way into a relationship with God; we either trust God, or we don't.

This verse in Romans sums it up well:

> However, to the one who does not work but trusts God who justifies the ungodly, their faith is credited as righteousness. (Romans 4:5)

4. According to this verse, what happens to the person who does not work but trusts God?

5. What does it mean to "not work" but "trust God" instead? What does that look like?

6. Does that mean we can sin as much as we want? (see Romans 6:1-4)

7. What does it mean for those who trust God when their faith is "credited as righteousness"?

Paul was writing this to make it absolutely clear that religion and behavior doesn't save us. A bunch of religious people during that time were living as if their lists of do's and don'ts—and how well they performed—made them right before God. Paul wanted to squash that common belief: *It's only by faith that we're made right before God.*

These religious people were big believers in Abraham from the book of Genesis. So Paul used Abraham and quoted Genesis to prove his point that it's faith that saves us. Here's what Paul wrote before the previous verses:

> [1] What then shall we say that Abraham, our forefather according to the flesh, discovered in this matter? [2] If, in fact, Abraham was justified by works, he had something to boast about—but not before God. [3] What does Scripture say? "Abraham believed God, and it was credited to him as righteousness."
> [4] Now to the one who works, wages are not credited as a gift but as an obligation. [5] However, to the one who does not work but trusts God who justifies the ungodly, their faith is credited as righteousness. (Romans 4:1-5)

Paul quotes Genesis: "Abraham believed God, and it was credited to him as righteousness," making the point that faith and trust in

God saves us, not our works. If it were our works, then we could boast about how "good" we are. No. It was Abraham's faith that saved him, not his good deeds—and the same applies to us today.

Because people are still trying to "earn" God's favor through being "good" rather than humbling themselves, they're not admitting the fact that they're not good enough; they're not putting their trust in God.

A recent Barna Group study reveals that most people "still place strong responsibility on human effort and choice regarding their ultimate destiny." (*What Americans Believe About Universalism and Pluralism*, Barna Group, April 18, 2011) It seems as though the majority of people still believe that if we're simply good enough, we'll probably go to heaven. And sadly that means Somebody has to draw a line that determines who makes it and who doesn't. And how is that decided? Sure, murderers don't make it—of course. But what if you just stole some stuff a couple of times? What about lying? Cheating? Laughing at that irritating kid in math class? Gossiping? How bad is too bad? Because we'd better be careful to not cross that line!

Thankfully, that's not how it works.

As we share our faith with our friends, let's remember to do just that—share our "faith." Let's share about our authentic "faith" . . . not some religion where we have to earn credits by trying to be good enough.

In today's session we'll talk more about what this looks like.

A MOMENT TO PRAY
Let's talk to God about this.

Talking to God is simple. We just want to get alone and get real with God just like Jesus tells us in Matthew, chapter 6.

Take a minute and specifically pray for the real conversations we'll have with our friends about our faith. Pray that God will help us not only to live out authentic faith, but also to talk about what real faith looks like.

LARGE GROUP TIME

Do this section with your group: Here's the section of this training that we'll do together with a group of believers.

OPTIONAL ICEBREAKER
Your leader will take us through a fun activity to break the ice during this large group time.

WATCH SECTION 4 OF DVD
A quick word from Jonathan: Now you get another chance to hear what I have to say and see an example of someone sharing faith with a friend. Watch SECTION 4 of the DVD right now where we'll finally take a peek at what putting our faith into words looks like.

GROUP ACTIVITY
Your leader will take us through an activity to help us process what we just learned.

SMALL GROUP DISCUSSION QUESTIONS
Think About This: In the video, Jonathan shows us three ways how *not* to share our faith.

    1. What were some of those ways?

2. Why was the "PRESENTATION" method so creepy?

3. What was wrong with the "SCARE TACTICS" method?

4. What about the example of the person who tried to "WING IT"? Why doesn't that work?

5. Did you come close to any of those methods when you tried to share with your partner a moment ago?

6. What could you do to be better prepared to share your faith story?

Read the following four Scriptures:

"Whoever believes in the Son has eternal life, but whoever rejects the Son will not see life, for God's wrath remains on them." (John 3:36)

"Very truly I tell you, whoever hears my word and believes him who sent me has eternal life and will not be judged but has crossed over from death to life." (John 5:24)

"Very truly I tell you, the one who believes has eternal life." (John 6:47)

However, to the one who does not work but trusts God who justifies the ungodly, their faith is credited as righteousness. (Romans 4:5)

7. What are some elements that all these verses have in common?

8. How many verses use the word *believe*? What does it mean?

9. The Romans verse uses the word *trust*. Do you think there's much of a difference between *trust* and *believe*?

10. What does the "believing" or "trusting" actually look like in your life?

11. Which of these verses might be good for you to include when explaining what it means to truly put your trust in Jesus?

SMALL GROUP WRAP-UP

We want to be ready when the Holy Spirit opens a door for us to share with our friends. One of the best ways we can be ready is to get to know Jesus better by reading his Word.

SOMETHING YOU CAN DO THIS WEEK

Let's spend some time in the Bible this week getting to know Jesus better so we can better articulate our faith.

In the video, when Ashley shares her faith story, she accurately answers several of Natalie's tough questions about belief and why Jesus saved us. Could you articulate your faith using words like Ashley does?

When we practiced our faith story with our friends, some of us might have had a little trouble explaining what "putting our trust in Jesus" actually looks like according to the Bible. Ashley presents the gospel message clearly, using examples from Scripture. The following are four facts Ashley presents that might be good to memorize. Notice that Ashley doesn't "list" these four facts; instead she makes sure that her faith story includes them.

Memorize these four facts this week, look up the Scriptures that support them, and then memorize at least one verse to correspond with each fact.

1. God loves us and wants a relationship with us. (John 3:16-17; Romans 5:8)

2. Our sin hurts us, hurts others, and messes up our relationship with God. (Romans 3:23; 6:23)

3. Only Jesus can save us from the problem of sin. (John 1:12; 14:6; Romans 3:22; 1 John 5:11-12)

4. If we want God's free gift of love and grace, we need to respond in faith, putting our trust in Jesus. (John 5:24; 6:47; Acts 3:19; Romans 4:5)

At the end of this week, get together with a Christian friend and practice telling your faith story again. This time try to include these four facts in your explanation of how someone puts his/her trust in Jesus.

FINAL THOUGHTS

Sharing your faith isn't easy. It starts with our own changed lives and then requires us to humbly and daily depend on God for strength and direction. When a door is opened, we don't want to err on the side of pushiness or silence, so it helps to listen and be a good friend while preparing to share our faith story.

A few years ago I encouraged my youth ministry leaders to undertake the same task I just asked you to undertake. I asked them to memorize those four steps, memorize four corresponding verses, and practice sharing the gospel with a Christian friend or loved one in the next week. Kevin did this and was really surprised with the result.

Growing up Kevin's family didn't go to church much. His mom went with him occasionally and always was an encouragement to him. When I gave Kevin this assignment, he decided to ask his mom if he could practice sharing the gospel with her. She was happy to help.

Kevin sat down with her that night and went through all four steps, sharing Scripture along the way. When he got to the final step, he said, "What do you think?" He was hoping to get some feedback on whether he did a good job or not. Instead, she said, "I need that."

Kevin was confused. "Need what?"

"I need to do what you said," she elaborated. "I've never done that. I've never responded like that."

Kevin was taken by surprise. "Oh . . . well okay."

That night Kevin's mom prayed and put her trust in Christ for the first time. The next Sunday she came to church with him.

I'm always amazed at the power of the gospel message when we have the opportunity to share it. Maybe that's why Paul said this in the first chapter of Romans:

> [16] For I am not ashamed of the gospel, because it is the power of God that brings salvation to everyone who believes: first to the Jew, then to the Gentile. [17] For in the gospel the righteousness of God is revealed—a righteousness that is by faith from first to last, just as it is written: "The righteous will live by faith." (Romans 1:16-17)

Take a moment and look back at your friends' names you wrote down in SESSION 2 of this book. Now . . . are you ready for real conversations about your faith?

LEADER'S
GUIDE

LEADERS...TRUST ME! YOU'LL REALLY WANT TO TAKE 45 SECONDS TO READ THIS INTRO!

I'm a big believer in keeping things simple. And we designed this leader's guide with the intent to make it very simple for you.

Here's how to use this leader's guide:

Up to this point in this book, everything has been for students (participants) to read and fill out. But from this point on, everything is geared toward your use.

We decided the best way to make the Leader's Guide easy to use was starting with an exact copy of the Participant's Guide and then adding very noticeable leader notes, transition statements, activity descriptions, etc.

We made these leader sections noticeable by shading them like this. So every time you see a shaded section, you know you're supposed to say or do something.

The non-shaded sections are what the students see in their Participant's Guide.

For example, whenever there is an Icebreaker activity you're supposed to lead, that area will be shaded like this.

Whenever there is an introduction statement or transition statement that you are supposed to say, that area will be shaded like this.

Whenever there is a group activity for you to lead, that area will be shaded.

If it's shaded, pay attention. The camera's rolling, and it's pointed at you!

Oh, and we've shaded one more area for you that's actually in the Participant's Guide: the small group questions. We decided to include them in the participant's guide so your students can take notes or answer the questions if they want. But we shaded those questions in the leader's guide as a cue that you need to lead the group through those questions.

One last piece of advice: Some of us are last-minute planners. Even if that's you, we really encourage you to read through your leader notes at least once prior to leading that session. Most of these sessions require a little bit of planning, and sometimes even a few props or supplies. So you'll want to be prepared for those moments.

That's it! Enjoy this guide. I think you'll find it helpful.

OUR
FAITH

AN AUTHENTIC FAITH
OPENING DOORS TO
REAL CONVERSATIONS

ALONE TIME

Grab a pen and read this section while you're alone.

SCARED SILENT

In this training we're tackling a scary subject for some of us: *Sharing our faith*. I'll be the first to admit it's scary for me. (If you haven't looked at the READ THIS FIRST section at the beginning of this book, quickly read it now—I believe you'll be relieved by what I have to say.)

Some of us might have some big fears when it comes to sharing our faith. Maybe we don't know what to say. Maybe we're afraid to bring it up because our friends have seen how imperfect we are. Sadly, sometimes these fears scare us silent.

That's why we're gonna look at these fears right now . . . and sidekick them in the face! (Sorry, sometimes I get a little bit expressive.)

This guide not only will help us sort through these fears and feelings, but also it will equip us to live out an authentic faith, which will open doors to authentic conversations.

I believe you'll really enjoy this!

WHAT ABOUT YOU?

Take a moment and write down your feelings about sharing your faith with others. I'll ask you a few candid questions, and you write down your answers. (This is just between you and God. No one else will see this.)

1. What's your biggest fear about sharing your faith with your friends?

2. What would make it easier for you to share your faith with your friends?

The Apostle Paul—after all of his religious rearing and training—knew he couldn't depend on his own wisdom and power to talk to others about God. He explained this in one of his letters to the church in Corinth:

> [1]And so it was with me, brothers and sisters. When I came to you, I did not come with eloquence or human wisdom as I proclaimed to you the testimony about God. [2]For I resolved to know nothing while I was with you except Jesus Christ and him crucified. [3]I came to you in weakness with great fear and trembling. [4]My message and my preaching were not with wise and persuasive words, but with a demonstration of the Spirit's power, [5]so that your faith might not rest on human wisdom, but on God's power. (1 Corinthians 2:1-5)

3. What are the some of the words Paul used in verse 3 to describe how he approached the people of Corinth?
4. What's the one thing Paul resolved to know, mentioned in verse 2?
5. What was the source of his power for his message and preaching, mentioned in verse 4?

As smart as Paul was, he knew he shouldn't get cocky and rely on his own abilities. Paul knew his wisdom and fancy words were nothing compared to God's power. So he decided to focus only on the message of Christ on the cross, giving Jesus all the attention and all the credit. Paul basically said, "It wasn't because of my good preaching and slick presentation that you guys were convinced; it was by God's power."

6. Why would it be smarter to rely on God rather than our own abilities?
7. What elements of human wisdom do you sometimes rely on?
8. What would be a way that you could rely on God's power instead of human wisdom?

In this section of Paul's letter to the Corinthians, he makes it clear that he didn't come to them with any eloquence or wisdom; instead he came in weakness and fear. This evident weakness made it clear to others that Paul was relying on God's power, not his own strength or street smarts! In other words, when people looked at Paul, they didn't see a really smart guy—they saw a guy whom God was working through. The focus was on God, not Paul.

> 9. What would this look like in your life? (pointing to God, not yourself)

A MOMENT TO PRAY

Let's talk to God about this.

Talking to God is simple. You don't need to use any magic words. In Matthew, chapter 6, Jesus told his disciples just to go into their rooms, close their doors, and be real with God who sees everything unseen anyway (so we might as well be real with God—who knows everything about us anyway).

So let's do that now. Take a minute and pray specifically that we can rely on God's power instead of our own wisdom in the way we detailed in question #8. Let's also pray that we can live out an authentic faith that will point other people to God.

LARGE GROUP TIME

Do this section with your group: I find it helpful to talk with other Christians and discuss life and receive encouragement to live out my faith in Jesus. That's why we're going to do much of this training as a group.

OPTIONAL ICEBREAKER

Your leader will take us through a fun activity to break the ice during this large group time.

INTRODUCTION STATEMENT— LEADERS SAY THIS

Today we're kicking off a four-week series titled, Real Conversations: Sharing Your Faith without Being Pushy.

I am so excited about these next four weeks because personally . . . (*Share an example from your own life that explains why you're excited about an evangelism series that emphasizes how authentic faith opens doors to authentic conversations.*)

Each week we're going to start off with something fun.

HUMAN MACHINE

(no supplies necessary)

This week let's kick it off with a creative little activity that we have to figure out together as teams.

Let's divide into teams now.

(If you have fewer than 10 people in your group, you'll create one "machine" as a group. If you have more than 10, you'll want to divide into teams of 10 to 20 people and have each team create a machine.)

The instructions are simple: *Make a human machine using all your team members.* Choose an appliance, machine, or contraption of any kind and act out all its parts with all the members of your team. For example: If you were to choose an electric toothbrush, several people could lie on the ground as handles; others could be vibrating bristles. Or you could choose a ski lift and have kids get scooped up by other team members locking arms. The sky's the limit . . . as long as you use every single team member!

(It's best to let them come up with their own ideas. But a few more great ones are a pinball machine—with a kid rolling around as the ball—a washing machine, or a car wash.)

(Give each group 5 to 10 minutes to brainstorm and organize its machine, then have each team present it to the group.)

TRANSITION STATEMENT—LEADERS SAY THIS

That was awesome seeing you all work together with one purpose.

Now we'll watch a DVD from a guy you're really going to enjoy. Watch this!

WATCH SECTION 1 OF DVD

A quick word from Jonathan: Hey! This is cool. You've been reading what I asked you to read! Now you get to hear what I have to say. Watch SECTION 1 of the DVD right now as we talk about how sharing our faith begins with . . . *our own faith!*

GROUP ACTIVITY

Your leader will take us through an activity to help us process what we just learned.

TRANSITION STATEMENT—LEADERS SAY THIS

The message of this session was clear: Authentic faith opens doors to authentic conversations.

For those of us who've made Christ the Lord of our lives, this affects two areas: Our ACTIONS and our WORDS. Living out authentic faith and being prepared for conversations about our faith.

The verse Jonathan read clearly exemplifies those two areas of our lives. Now I want us to take a closer look at what this might look like for us day to day.

Everyone divide into groups consisting of 4 to 8 students and one leader. All the groups will stay in the same room during this exercise, then report their findings to the large group.

SMALL GROUP EXERCISE— LED BY SMALL GROUP LEADER

(have a pen and some 3x5 cards ready)

Now that you're in your groups, I want you to read 1 Peter 3:15-16 and write down as many elements of these verses as you can—but one element per card, kind of like the elements Jonathan listed on the screen. *(But maybe have them read it in different translations.)*

> **Note to Leaders:** Hand them 10 blank cards. Help them come up with at least these 7 elements:

- Revere Christ as Lord
- Be prepared to answer
- Someone asks you
- Give the reason
- Have hope
- Someone notices your hope
- Good behavior

Now as a group let's move these cards around and place these key elements of this passage in sequential order, as they would happen in real life. Okay . . . what happens first? What's next? Organize the cards in order from top to bottom and be able to explain what this process might look like in the world of today's teenagers.

> **Note to Leaders:** Once the cards are in order, place one super-long piece of tape down on all the cards so you can hold them up and show your order of elements to the group.

Now present your findings to the large group. When you present, do the following:

Show us the sequence you chose and quickly explain your reasoning.

Answer this question: What would this process look like in the world of today's teenagers?

ACTIVITY WRAP-UP

When we broke the verses down, it helped us see that the process of sharing our faith begins when we truly make Christ LORD of our lives. As others see the hope that Christ provides, we'll have opportunities to engage in conversations about Jesus. Let's be prepared for those conversations so we can share *the reason* for the hope within us!

Let's talk about this further in our small groups.

SMALL GROUP DISCUSSION QUESTIONS

Think About This: Many of us might get a little uncomfortable when we talk about sharing our faith. Maybe it's because we know that it has a lot to do with how we live out our own faith. Maybe it's because we're just scared of having conversations about our faith with our friends. Either way . . . you're not alone. Most of us probably feel scared and ill-equipped at times.

1. Some of us might have had some bad experiences or witnessed some really negative examples of people telling others about Jesus. Does anyone want to share one of those experiences?

2. Many of us have probably encountered people with very genuine faith in Jesus—so real that you almost wanted to ask them about it. Does someone want to share what you saw in this person that made you think, "I'd like a faith like that" or "If I had questions about my faith, I'd want to talk with her"?

3. Jonathan introduced the session talking about the feelings, fears, or apprehensions many of us might feel if we found out that tomorrow one of our friends was going to ask us about our faith. Let's look at our feelings honestly for a moment: How would you feel right now if you knew that tomorrow you'd have to share your faith with a friend? Why would you feel like that?

In the verses we just studied, we learned that sharing our faith requires WORDS and ACTION. First, we live out our faith in our ACTIONS. And then those actions—that authentic faith, the "hope" others see in our lives—open the doors to conversations: WORDS.

4. What does it look like to do what the verse says and "revere Christ as Lord"?

5. In what ways might your friends see that authentic faith and "hope" in you?

6. What areas in your life right now might distract people from seeing that "hope" in you?

7. What can do to try to fix those distractions and live a more authentic life?

8. Are you ready to have conversations, explaining the reason for your hope? What would you say?

SMALL GROUP WRAP-UP

Hopefully this training we're doing together will help us not only to live out that hope of Christ in our lives, but also to prepare us for those real conversations. As we continue this training, we'll talk a little bit more about how to articulate our faith.

SOMETHING YOU CAN DO THIS WEEK

We've just discussed the "hope" in our lives. This made us consider two areas:

1. Where friends see authentic faith and "hope" in our lives.
2. Areas where we're weak, and where our actions distract others from seeing the hope in our lives.

Let's start off each morning this week in prayer and pray about those two specific areas of our lives. Pray that God will help us, continue to work through us, and reveal himself to others through our actions. Also pray that God will help us get rid of the "sin that so easily entangles [us]." (Hebrews 12:1-2)

OUR MISSION FIELD

THE PEOPLE YOU ENCOUNTER DAY TO DAY

ALONE TIME

Grab a pen and read this section while you're alone.

THE PEOPLE YOU ENCOUNTER
In the last session we discussed how "sharing our faith" begins with our own faith. Hopefully for the last week you've been praying and asking God to help you live an authentic faith.

An authentic faith will open the door to real conversations with the people we encounter each day.

Today we're going to take a closer look at the types of people we will encounter.

WHAT ABOUT YOU?
Take a moment and think about two or three friends with whom you might want to share your faith. Ask yourself who you'd like to talk to if you knew that, for whatever reason, you and your friends would actually have a pleasant conversation about your faith. Write their names in the blanks provided.

Friends I want to reach out to:

_____

_____

_____

Over the next few weeks we'll specifically pray for these friends and ask God to reveal himself through us so we might have an opportunity to live out our faith and maybe even dialogue about it with our friends. Pray that our friends might be willing to listen and receive what we have to say, too.

In the book of Matthew, Jesus talks about how people receive our message. He cleverly tells it in the form of a parable.

[1] That same day Jesus went out of the house and sat by the lake.
[2] Such large crowds gathered around him that he got into a boat and sat in it, while all the people stood on the shore. [3] Then he told them many things in parables, saying: "A farmer went out to sow his seed. [4] As he was scattering the seed, some fell along the path, and the birds came and ate it up. [5] Some fell on rocky places, where it did not have much soil. It sprang up quickly, because the soil was shallow. [6] But when the sun came up, the plants were scorched, and they withered because they had no root. [7] Other seed fell among thorns, which grew up and choked the plants.
[8] Still other seed fell on good soil, where it produced a crop—a hundred, sixty or thirty times what was sown. (Matthew 13:1-8)

1. What do you suppose the seed represents?
2. What do you suppose the different soils represent?

Jesus goes on to explain the parable a few verses later:

[18] "Listen then to what the parable of the sower means: [19] When anyone hears the message about the kingdom and does not understand it, the evil one comes and snatches away what was sown in their heart. This is the seed sown along the path. [20] The seed falling on rocky ground refers to someone who hears the word and at once receives it with joy. [21] But since they have no root, they last only a short time. When trouble or persecution comes because of the word, they quickly fall away. [22] The seed falling among the thorns refers to someone who hears the word, but the worries of this life and the deceitfulness of wealth choke the word, making it unfruitful. [23] But the seed falling on good soil refers to someone who hears the word and understands it. This is the one who produces a crop, yielding a hundred, sixty or thirty times what was sown." (Matthew 13:18-23)

Jesus explains that the sower shares "messages about the kingdom" (the seed). People (the soils) receive these seeds in different ways.

3. Describe a person who's like the path.

4. Describe a person who's like the rocky ground.

5. Describe a person who's like the thorns.

6. Describe a person who's like the good soil.

7. Which of these soils have you observed at your school and in your group of friends?

I always find it interesting that, in this parable, the sower doesn't sow different kinds of seeds. The seeds are all the *same message* about the kingdom. The difference is in the *soil*—the person receiving the message.

In other words, the people we encounter will always receive God's message differently. This session will hopefully prepare us for encountering these various people.

A MOMENT TO PRAY

Let's talk to God about this.

In the last session I mentioned that talking to God is simple. We just want to get alone and get real with God just like Jesus told us in Matthew, chapter 6.

Let's do that now. Take a minute and specifically pray for the friends we just wrote about here, and ask God to reveal himself through us so we might have opportunities to live out our faith and maybe even dialogue about it with these friends.

Do this section with your group: Here's the section of this training that we'll do together with a group of believers.

OPTIONAL ICEBREAKER

Your leader will take us through a fun activity to break the ice during this large group time.

INTRODUCTION STATEMENT—
LEADERS SAY THIS

Today we're continuing our four-week series, Real Conversations: Sharing Your Faith without Being Pushy.

Each week we'll start it off with something fun.

GET ON BOARD

(Make available several 2x4s, maybe 8- to 10-feet long each—long enough for a team of teenagers to stand upon. You'll need as many boards as you have teams—enough for everyone on each team to be standing on its board.)

This week let's kick it off with a fun little activity that we have to complete by working together.

(Lay boards on the ground and divide into teams.)

Each team get all of your team members on your board.

Now, without talking or using any hand signals, organize

yourselves by birth date, from January 1 to December 31. *(Point to one side of each team's board)* This side of the board is January 1.

Go!

Remember, no communication at all. Just go where you think you stand.

(Let each team organize itself until the team is finished.)

Now . . . let's see how accurately we all guessed! Everyone tell your birthday to the people next to you, then readjust your places if need be.

Interesting, huh?

Consider this: *If we never take time to listen to the people next to us, we'll never know where we stand.*

TRANSITION STATEMENT—LEADERS SAY THIS

Go back to your own seats now.

See how difficult it is to determine where people are without communicating with them? This is something to consider as we think about getting to know the people we encounter each day.

Now we're going to watch a DVD again. Listen to what Jonathan says about the people we encounter day to day.

Watch this!

WATCH SECTION 2 OF DVD

A quick word from Jonathan: Now you get another chance to hear what I have to say. Watch SECTION 2 of the DVD right now as we talk about our mission field, the people we encounter day to day.

GROUP ACTIVITY

Your leader will take us through an activity to help us process what we just learned.

TRANSITION STATEMENT—LEADERS SAY THIS

Jonathan just introduced us to six types of kids. Let's take a closer look at how we can actually reach out to and/or disciple each of these kids day to day.

I'll need six volunteers! I'll call you up one at a time.

Note to Leaders: Have six signs ready (simple pieces of bright paper or cardstock with words printed in a large font) that say: NO WAY, NOT INTERESTED, CHECKING THINGS OUT, STAGNANT, GROWING, LOOKING FOR MINISTRY. Place six chairs in front of the room so you can line up the six types of kids exactly as they were lined up in the video. Hand each kid the appropriate sign as they each sit up front. Now lead some discussion in the following manner:

Let me start by choosing three people to be our "OUTREACH kids."

I need a NO WAY kid. *(Hand kid sign and have him sit up front in appropriate chair.)* How many of you have met NO WAY kids? Why do you suppose they have this attitude?

Now I need a NOT INTERESTED kid. *(Hand kid sign and have her sit up front in appropriate chair.)* How many of you have met NOT INTERESTED kids?

Now a CHECKING THINGS OUT kid. *(Hand kid sign and have him sit up front in appropriate chair.)* How many of you have met CHECKING THINGS OUT kids?

These are our three OUTREACH kids. They don't know Jesus yet. Why? Were any of you ever in these categories? *(Allow a few students to answer.)*

Note to Leaders: We're hoping to simply help students in our group process the fact that these three OUTREACH kids don't yet know Jesus. Maybe these OUTREACH kids don't know Jesus because they're bitter for some reason, or maybe they just would rather live for the moment, or maybe they're looking for answers, and they just need someone to introduce them to Jesus.

Now let me choose three people to represent our "SPIRITUAL GROWTH kids."

I need a STAGNANT kid. *(Hand kid sign and have her sit up front in appropriate chair.)* How many of you have met STAGNANT kids?

Now I need a GROWING kid. *(Hand kid sign and have him sit up front in appropriate chair.)* How many of you know GROWING kids? How many of you believe you might be a GROWING kid?

And finally, I need a LOOKING FOR MINISTRY kid. *(Hand kid sign and have her sit up front in appropriate chair.)* How many of you know LOOKING FOR MINISTRY kids? How many of you believe you might be a LOOKING FOR MINISTRY kid?

These are our three SPIRITUAL GROWTH kids. At one time or another, each of these kids put their trust in Jesus, asking him to forgive their sins and start transforming their lives.

So then . . . why are each of these three kids so different spiritually? *(Allow a few students to answer.)*

Note to Leaders: We're hoping to help students think about the fact that different kids are at different stages of growth in their spiritual journeys. Soon we'll discuss how to help each of these kids in these different stages.

Now, let's think about how we can meet each of these kids' spiritual needs.

Let's start with the NO WAY kid. How do you reach him/her?

> **Note to Leaders:** Usually kids will answer, "Invite him to church." Then I turn to the crowd and say, "If we invite a NO WAY kid to church, how will he respond?" The crowd inevitably says, "NO WAY!" Then I re-ask the question: "So how do you reach him/her?"

What about the NOT INTERESTED kid—how do you reach him/her?

What about the CHECKING THINGS OUT kid—how do you reach him/her?

> **Note to Leaders:** We're trying to help students think through how to reach out to these different types of kids. Good answers will include elements such as: "Loving them for who they are," and "befriending them," and "as the situation permits, engaging in spiritual conversations." Your students shouldn't have all the answers, but one thing leaders can do is encourage students that the next sessions will help them with this very issue ...

All three types of kids need Jesus. Hopefully as we befriend these kids and live authentic lives, that will open the door to spiritual conversations where we can tell them about a relationship with Jesus.

Now let's look at the three SPIRITUAL GROWTH kids. They need to grow in their faith.

How do you help the STAGNANT kid grow?

How do you help the GROWING kid grow?

And does the LOOKING FOR MINISTRY kid need to grow? (Absolutely!) How can many of us who are in the LOOKING FOR MINISTRY category help other LOOKING FOR MINISTRY kids grow?

ACTIVITY WRAP-UP

As you can see, all these kids have spiritual needs. The three OUT-REACH kids need to know Jesus. It seems the best way to give them opportunities to do that is by being a friend and living out an authentic faith. As we learned last week, if we live out the hope in our lives, we might have opportunities to have real conversations with them and tell them the reason for the hope that is within us.

Let's divide into small groups and talk about this further.

SMALL GROUP DISCUSSION QUESTIONS

Think About This: In the video we heard Jesus' commission to his followers, asking them (and us) to go and make disciples. Jonathan said this could be said like this: *"While you're at home, school, sports, and with friends . . . as you're doing life day to day . . . make a conscious effort to make disciples."*

1. Of those places (home, school, sports, hanging with friends after school), which makes it the most difficult to think about this process of discipleship—reaching out to our friends and meeting their spiritual needs? Why is this difficult?
2. Which of the three types of OUTREACH kids is the hardest to reach? Why?
3. What do you suppose is the *worst* way to reach out to them?
4. What do you suppose is a *good* way to try to reach out to them?
5. Which of the three types of OUTREACH kids is the easiest to reach? Why?
6. How do you reach out to them?

SMALL GROUP WRAP-UP

I will hand each of you a 3x5 card and pen. I want you to think of someone you know who's an OUTREACH kid. Write his or her name on this card. Now I want you to think of some of the good ideas you've heard in our discussion and around this group today that might help you take the first steps toward reaching out to this person. Write down one idea of something you can do this week.

Does anyone want to share your idea around the group?

Let's close and pray specifically for each of these kids we want to reach out to this week.

SOMETHING YOU CAN DO THIS WEEK

We've just taken a detailed look at our mission field—the people we encounter each day at home, school, sports, while hanging with friends . . . wherever! We realize these people may receive God's message differently from the way we receive it.

Let's start off each morning this week specifically praying for the people whose names we wrote down in the beginning of this session. Let's pray that we continue to live an authentic faith that might open the door to real conversations with these people.

OUR
APPROACH

WHEN ACTIONS OPEN
DOORS FOR WORDS

ALONE TIME

Grab a pen and read this section while you're alone.

TIMING IS EVERYTHING

In the last session we took a detailed look at our mission field—the people we encounter each day at home, school, sports, while hanging with friends . . . wherever! We also wrote down the names of three friends we want to reach out to with God's message of love and grace. Hopefully we've been praying about this for the last week.

Today we'll start thinking about how we approach conversations with these friends. After all, we don't want to be pushy—but at the same time we want to be bold and look for open doors to have real conversations.

Now let me tell you what we're *not* going to do. We won't memorize some sales pitch and randomly try to force it on people. This does more harm than good.

Think about it: Someone may know *how* to present the gospel message, all kinds of cool stories and illustrations, and even convincing methods of persuasion. But it doesn't matter how good the presentation is if the presenters don't have any sense of *when* to present it.

Over a decade of marriage to my wife, I've learned a lot about listening.

Unfortunately I've learned most of it the hard way. In our first year of marriage, Lori would come home from a hard day and share a problem she faced. I, being the man with all the answers, was gracious enough to solve those problems for her—explaining what she did wrong and what she needed to do in the future. After several experiences of sleeping on the couch I realized, "Hey . . . she doesn't want answers! She just wants someone to *listen* to her!"

Sometimes people just need someone to *listen*. Sometimes people just need a friend. Being a friend will open the door in God's timing. God will provide a number of opportunities for you to share your faith with your friends. Presenting the gospel is the easy part; the tough part is knowing *when* and finding those open doors.

So let's dive in and discuss our approach.

WHAT ABOUT YOU?

Take a moment and think about the names of the friends you wrote down in the last session.

1. Have you ever had an opportunity to share your faith with these friends or others in the past? How did you approach the subject?
2. Have you ever witnessed someone being too pushy while sharing about Jesus? What should that person have done differently?

Jesus constantly found himself in situations in which the subject of God, faith, or eternal life emerged. Jesus never seemed pushy, yet he brought up the subject quite frequently. One example is when he went into Samaria with his disciples. Most of the religious people tried to avoid Samaria—they didn't like the Samaritans at all. But Jesus saw this as an opportunity to talk with some people who were often ignored.

[4] Now he had to go through Samaria. [5] So he came to a town in Samaria called Sychar, near the plot of ground Jacob had given to his son Joseph. [6] Jacob's well was there, and Jesus, tired as he was from the journey, sat down by the well. It was about noon.
[7] When a Samaritan woman came to draw water, Jesus said to her, "Will you give me a drink?" [8] (His disciples had gone into the town to buy food.)
[9] The Samaritan woman said to him, "You are a Jew and I am a

Samaritan woman. How can you ask me for a drink?" (For Jews
do not associate with Samaritans.)
[10] Jesus answered her, "If you knew the gift of God and who it
is that asks you for a drink, you would have asked him and he
would have given you living water."
[11] "Sir," the woman said, "you have nothing to draw with and
the well is deep. Where can you get this living water? [12] Are you
greater than our father Jacob, who gave us the well and drank
from it himself, as did also his sons and his livestock?"
[13] Jesus answered, "Everyone who drinks this water will be thirsty
again, [14] but whoever drinks the water I give them will never
thirst. Indeed, the water I give them will become in them a spring
of water welling up to eternal life."
[15] The woman said to him, "Sir, give me this water so that I won't
get thirsty and have to keep coming here to draw water." (John
4:4-15)

3. Most of the religious people of the day didn't associate with
   Samaritans. Why do you suppose Jesus decided to visit
   Samaria and start a conversation with this woman?
4. How do you suppose this woman felt when Jesus started talking with her?
5. Is there a place you could go to start conversations with
   people who're typically ignored or overlooked?
6. Jesus and the woman talked about water, and the next thing
   we know, he was having a spiritual conversation with the
   woman! How did he do that?
7. Why do you suppose this woman was so interested in what
   Jesus had to say?

In this Bible passage, Jesus talks about "living water" and
quenching thirst to get this woman's attention. As we read the
entire passage, this woman wasn't only thirsty physically—she was
thirsty *spiritually*. Many people we encounter might be thirsting
for something to fill the emptiness in their lives. God frequently
opens doors for us to offer hope to people in these otherwise hopeless situations.

A MOMENT TO PRAY

Let's talk to God about this.

In the last couple of sessions I mentioned that talking to God is simple. We just want to get alone and get real with God, just like Jesus told us in Matthew, chapter 6.

Let's do that now. Take a minute and specifically pray for opportunities to reach out to people who are often ignored or overlooked. Let's also pray for Spirit-led boldness to share the truth in these situations—but without being pushy.

Do this section with your group: Here's the section of this training that we'll do together with a group of believers.

OPTIONAL ICEBREAKER
Your leader will take us through a fun activity to break the ice during this large group time.

INTRODUCTION STATEMENT— LEADERS SAY THIS
Today we're continuing our four-week series, Real Conversations: Sharing Your Faith without Being Pushy.

Let's kick off this week with something fun.

THE AMAZING SALESPERSON
(Only necessary props are a roll of toilet paper placed inside a good-sized box so that the salesperson has no idea what's inside the box.)

I need a volunteer who's an amazing salesperson. This person can sell a freezer to a scientist on Antarctica.

(Choose a volunteer who's quick and could be a good salesperson. Note: You also might want to choose someone who hasn't already turned to the back of the book and read this activity!)

This salesperson is so good that he/she can sell anything! As a matter of fact, he/she can even sell something when he/she doesn't know what it is.

So here's what I'm going to do. I'm going to step behind him/her right now and show you what's in this box. All of you in the audience need to keep totally quiet and not tell our salesperson what's in the box *(open the box and show the roll of toilet paper to the group, but don't show the salesperson).*

Now it's time for our salesperson to pitch us about how good this item is. Sure, he/she doesn't know what's in the box, but that doesn't matter. The salesperson is *that* good at selling . . . anything.

(To the salesperson) Go ahead and give us your sales pitch!

(The volunteer does his/her best to give a generic sales pitch; it's usually pretty funny.)

Now I have a few questions for you about this product, then I'm going to open it up to the group members so they can ask you questions, too.

- When do you find it most necessary to use this product?
- Who are you usually with when you use this product?
- After you use this product, what do you do with it?

Group members . . . do you have any questions?

(Leave time for group member questions.)

I believe it's time to show our salesperson what he/she was trying to sell!

(Show salesperson the toilet paper.)

Let's give him/her a round of applause. Great job!

TRANSITION STATEMENT—LEADERS SAY THIS

That was . . . *gross!* But we got to see some crazy sales skills from *(our volunteer).*

I've met some good salespeople, and I've met some lousy ones. For example, when it's dinnertime and some pushy salesperson calls and won't take "no" for an answer—nobody likes products or ideas pushed on them.

Sadly, some Christians have the reputation of being pushy.

Is that the only way to share our faith?

Tonight we'll talk about our "approach." Let's watch the DVD again and listen to what Jonathan says about how we approach our conversations with our friends—without pushing them away.

Watch this.

WATCH SECTION 3 OF DVD

A quick word from Jonathan: Now you get another chance to hear what I have to say. Watch SECTION 3 of the DVD right now as we talk about how we approach conversations with our friends. After all, we don't want to be pushy, but at the same time we want to be bold and look for open doors to have real conversations.

GROUP ACTIVITY

Your leader will take us through an activity to help us process what was just presented.

TRANSITION STATEMENT—LEADERS SAY THIS

Think about that prayer that Jonathan encouraged us to pray as we start each day: "God, how can I represent you today in *word* and *action*?"

This Spirit-led approach isn't pushy . . . but it also isn't silent.

One of the best skills we can use with this balanced and caring approach is *listening*. Listening helps us focus on others' needs, not our own agenda. But good listeners also ask good questions.

We'll now try two simple activities that will help us focus on the other person and develop our listening skills.

NO I'S

Everybody stand up and grab a partner.

The instructions are simple. The two of you are to have a conversation for 1 minute . . . *without saying the word "I."* That's right. Neither of you can say the word "I" in your conversation.

Notice I said "conversation," which implies a two-way exchange. So make sure that each of you talks . . . but still, neither of you can say "I."

When one of you says "I," which many of you will, you *both* need to sit down. By the end of 1 minute we'll see which pairs are left standing.

Ready? Go!

(Time one minute. Usually more than half the pairs will end up sitting at one time or another during the minute. Tell them when one minute is up.)

Wow. We have quite a few people sitting! You couldn't get through a sentence without saying "I" . . . could you?

The point of this exercise was simple: We need to stop focusing on ourselves and work on becoming better listeners.

ECHO LISTENING

Let's try something else. This is called "echo listening."

The instructions are simple. In pairs, choose one of you to be the talker and the other person to be the listener. The talker begins, telling the listener something that happened to him/her recently. The talker can discuss a recent trip or something that happened in English class. It doesn't matter.

Here's the key: The listener guides the conversation by echoing words the talker says.

Here's how it works: As the talker begins the conversation, she might say, *"I went camping with my family last week in Yellowstone."*

The listener needs to simply echo one of those words and phrase it as a question, depending on the listener's interest. So in this case, if the listener is curious about Yellowstone, he should reply, *"Yellowstone?"*

If instead the listener is interested in the fact that the talker went with her family, he could reply, *"Family?"* The listener has the power to direct the conversation a little bit.

Now the talker responds and elaborates. Here's an example of how such a conversation might go:

> TALKER: "I went camping with my family last week in Yellowstone."
>
> LISTENER: "Camping?"
>
> TALKER: "Oh yeah. We love camping. My entire family goes three weekends a year."
>
> LISTENER: "Entire family?"
>
> TALKER: "Yep. My family, my Papa and Nana, and my dad's brother's family with their dogs."
>
> LISTENER: "Dogs?"

You get the idea.

So let's try that now. Talker, you tell something that happened recently; listener, you echo words phrased as questions.

Ready? Decide who will be the talker and who will be the echo listener.

Ready? Go!

(Let your group try it for 2 to 3 minutes. Walk around and judge how long you should let it go on. Then stop it and switch.)

Okay, now switch roles. The talker is now the listener, and vice versa.

Ready? Go!

(Let them try this for the same amount of time.)

Okay . . . let's stop. I'm going to tell you something very important: *This method, as you practiced it, is ridiculous!*

Seriously. No one has conversations like that.

But what this exercise did is help us practice *actually listening* to what people say to us and then engaging them to talk more about certain topics.

In reality, you'd probably use entire "echo" sentences. The conversation might sound more like:

TALKER: "I went camping with my family last week in
  Yellowstone."
LISTENER: "Oh, that's cool. Do you camp often?"
TALKER: "Oh yeah. We love camping. My entire family
  goes three weekends a year."
LISTENER: "Wow, your entire family?"
TALKER: "Yep. My family, my Papa and Nana, and my
  dad's brother's family with their dogs."
LISTENER: "Cool. Do you like dogs?"

ACTIVITY WRAP-UP

Here's the point: People who listen, care!

If you can become a good listener, people will talk with you.

Wherever Jesus went, he always seemed to care for people's needs first. He healed the sick; he fed the hungry. Jesus got the reputation for being a caring person, and quickly people began to come to him. What better way to start a conversation than when the conversation comes to you!

Our approach shouldn't be, "Hey, listen to me!" Instead we should care enough about others to listen, making them feel noticed and heard.

Let's divide into small groups and talk about this further.

SMALL GROUP DISCUSSION QUESTIONS

Think About This: In the video Jonathan talks about two extreme examples of how we approach our friends—both of them lousy ways to share our faith.

1. What are the two negative examples Jonathan gives?
2. Which extreme approach do you tend to gravitate toward? Why?

3. What's something you could do to avoid floating toward that extreme?

4. Jonathan says there's another, more balanced approach. What does he call this approach? Why do you suppose he calls it that?

5. How can you be more Spirit-led?

In 1 Peter 5:5-7, the apostle writes:

All of you, clothe yourselves with humility toward one another, because,
"God opposes the proud but shows favor to the humble."
6 Humble yourselves, therefore, under God's mighty hand, that he may lift you up in due time. 7 Cast all your anxiety on him because he cares for you.

In the video, Jonathan reminds us that throughout the Bible, God frequently tells us to "humble ourselves." God doesn't want us to make the mistake of trying to make it on our own; God wants us to depend on him.

6. According to 1 Peter 5:6, what happens when we humble ourselves?

7. How can you humble yourself—in other words, what does this look like in your life?

8. How do you suppose God might lift you up?

If the idea of sharing your faith scares you, then simply humble yourself.

God actually *wants* you to give him your worry and anxiety about this. Because when you're humble enough to do that, God will take care of you.

9. God wants us to rely on him at all times. How is this truth especially helpful to us when we're trying to engage in real conversations about our faith with our friends?

SMALL GROUP WRAP-UP

This "Spirit-led" approach isn't pushy . . . but it is bold.

As we live out our faith authentically, people will notice our actions. If we're humble enough to rely on God and let his Spirit give us boldness, God will open doors for real, honest conversations. They might start with us asking good questions and being ready to actually listen.

This whole process might seem scary at times. That's why it's reassuring to know that the Holy Spirit is right there with us, even giving us the right words to say.

I'm glad we're not in this alone!

SOMETHING YOU CAN DO THIS WEEK

The Spirit-led approach requires us to be good listeners—not just with our friends, but *with God's Spirit*. Sometimes the Holy Spirit might ask us to reach out to someone and care for that person. For example, maybe we'll see a homeless person who's asking for food; maybe we'll see a fellow student sitting alone on campus. God might prompt you to walk over and start a conversation with that person. We must be ready to listen and respond when God prompts us to show compassion. We must be ready to *actually listen* to the person to whom we're reaching out.

Let's start each morning this week in prayer and pray the words that Jonathan encourages us to pray: "God, how can I represent you today in *word* and *action*?" Let's pray these words every morning and then keep our ears ready to listen throughout the day. In addition, let's remember to keep praying for the three friends whose names we wrote down last week. Let's ask God to specifically help us represent him in word and action to those friends.

OUR
MESSAGE

SHARING THE REASON
FOR YOUR HOPE

ALONE TIME

Grab a pen and read this section while you're alone.

NOW WHAT?

For the last three weeks we've been discussing our faith, our mission field, and our approach. All of this has finally brought us to the point where we actually "talk" with our friends about our faith.

Now you might be wondering, "So what do I say?"

Think about this: Let's say you've already done everything we've been talking about so far:

OUR FAITH—You live out an authentic faith, allowing God to slowly rid you of those sins that so easily entangle you.

OUR MISSION FIELD—You think about the people you want to reach and pray for them daily.

OUR APPROACH—You look for opportunities to reach out to these people in word and action, listening to the Holy Spirit and paying attention to the Spirit's "nudges."

Now what?

Perhaps one of the friends you've been praying for opens up to you and gets real about his search for meaning in his life. You listen carefully to your friend, and the Holy Spirit "nudges" you to share your faith . . .

At this point, what do you say?

WHAT ABOUT YOU?

If you live out an authentic faith, the Holy Spirit will open doors to real conversations in which you have opportunities to share the reason for the hope that lives inside you. The question is, *What do you share?*

1. Have you ever had the opportunity to share your faith? If so, what happened?
2. Do you believe you explained your faith well enough? Why or why not?
3. What essentials do you believe people need to know about a relationship with God?

The more you read the Bible, the more you'll learn about what our relationship with God is all about. From the very beginning—in the book of Genesis—all the way until the time of Jesus, you'll see the same elements again and again: *God's love for us* coupled with *our decisions to trust in God . . . or not.*

That pretty much sums it up.

Over and over again, God loved people and communicated his desire to have a relationship with them. And people either trusted God or decided to do things their own way.

In the last few sessions we've been discussing what "trusting" God looks like in our own lives. An authentic faith doesn't mean we're perfect. But when we trust in Jesus, putting his words into practice, we begin to live more like him.

And don't underestimate the extent to which people around us notice this kind of authentic faith. Our friends are probably good at spotting "fake."

Young people today are pretty skeptical of religion in general. That's where true Christianity stands out from most "religion." Our relationship with God is based on faith, not how "good" we are (or aren't). As we share our faith with our friends, we should be sure to communicate this simple, biblical truth. We can't earn our way into a relationship with God; we either trust God, or we don't.

This verse in Romans sums it up well:

> However, to the one who does not work but trusts God who justifies the ungodly, their faith is credited as righteousness. (Romans 4:5)

4. According to this verse, what happens to the person who does not work but trusts God?

5. What does it mean to "not work" but "trust God" instead? What does that look like?

6. Does that mean we can sin as much as we want? (see Romans 6:1-4)

7. What does it mean for those who trust God when their faith is "credited as righteousness"?

Paul was writing this to make it absolutely clear that religion and behavior doesn't save us. A bunch of religious people during that time were living as if their lists of do's and don'ts—and how well they performed—made them right before God. Paul wanted to squash that common belief: *It's only by faith that we're made right before God.*

These religious people were big believers in Abraham from the book of Genesis. So Paul used Abraham and quoted Genesis to prove his point that it's faith that saves us. Here's what Paul wrote before the previous verses:

> [1] What then shall we say that Abraham, our forefather according to the flesh, discovered in this matter? [2] If, in fact, Abraham was justified by works, he had something to boast about—but not before God. [3] What does Scripture say? "Abraham believed God, and it was credited to him as righteousness."
> [4] Now to the one who works, wages are not credited as a gift but as an obligation. [5] However, to the one who does not work but trusts God who justifies the ungodly, their faith is credited as righteousness. (Romans 4:1-5)

Paul quotes Genesis: "Abraham believed God, and it was credited to him as righteousness," making the point that faith and trust in God saves us, not our works. If it were our works, then we could boast about how "good" we are. No. It was Abraham's faith that saved him, not his good deeds—and the same applies to us today.

Because people are still trying to "earn" God's favor through being "good" rather than humbling themselves, they're not admitting the fact that they're not good enough; they're not putting their trust in God.

A recent Barna Group study reveals that most people "still place strong responsibility on human effort and choice regarding their ultimate destiny." (*What Americans Believe About Universalism and Pluralism*, Barna Group, April 18, 2011) It seems as though the majority of people still believe that if we're simply good enough, we'll probably go to heaven. And sadly that means Somebody has to draw a line that determines who makes it and who doesn't. And how is that decided? Sure, murderers don't make it—of course. But what if you just stole some stuff a couple of times? What about lying? Cheating? Laughing at that irritating kid in math class? Gossiping? How bad is too bad? Because we'd better be careful to not cross that line!

Thankfully, that's not how it works.

As we share our faith with our friends, let's remember to do just that—share our "faith." Let's share about our authentic "faith" . . . not some religion where we have to earn credits by trying to be good enough.

In today's session we'll talk more about what this looks like.

A MOMENT TO PRAY

Let's talk to God about this.

Talking to God is simple. We just want to get alone and get real with God just like Jesus tells us in Matthew, chapter 6.

Take a minute and specifically pray for the real conversations we'll have with our friends about our faith. Pray that God will help us not only to live out authentic faith, but also to talk about what real faith looks like.

Do this section with your group: Here's the section of this training that we'll do together with a group of believers.

OPTIONAL ICEBREAKER

Your leader will take us through a fun activity to break the ice during this large group time.

INTRODUCTION STATEMENT— LEADERS SAY THIS

Today we are finishing up our four-week series, Real Conversations: Sharing Your Faith without Being Pushy.

Let's kick off this last week with something fun!

FAITH EGG WALK

(Supplies needed: A source of loud music, a blindfold, a few dozen eggs, and a big bag of peanuts. Set up a large open area as the "road" your volunteer will navigate, maybe 10 feet wide by at least 20 feet long. Place eggs as landmines all over the road. Spread them out so that a blindfolded person can make their way through the maze without stepping on the eggs.)

I need a volunteer with a lot of faith! *(I recommend a volunteer who isn't likely to start throwing the eggs at group members; a reserved kid is a much better option.)*

Okay, your task is simple: You just need to make it down this

20-foot road, stepping on the fewest number of eggs possible. The problem is, you'll need to listen to instructions from all your friends—except all of them will be talking at the same time! And your goal is to step on zero eggs.

Crowd, are you ready to yell out instructions to our volunteer?

Okay, are you ready? Cue the blindfold music!

(When the loud music starts, put the blindfold on the volunteer. Make sure you test the blindfold, making sure the volunteer can't see his/her feet. This is very important. Meanwhile, have a few pre-selected volunteers collect all the eggs and replace them with peanuts. Add a few more peanuts than there were eggs to make the path very difficult. Have your volunteers work quickly and quietly under the cover of the loud music.)

Okay . . . now that your blindfold is on, we're all going to guide you. Listen to everyone's voice, and we'll navigate you across!

Ready? Go!

(Your volunteer will try to go through the road, most likely stepping on several peanuts along the way thinking they're eggs. Continue to pump up the crowd to yell out a bunch of different commands for the volunteer to follow: "Left!" "Right!" "Get straight!" "Go forward!" "Move ahead!" When the volunteer gets halfway across, stop her.)

Okay, stop for a moment! You're halfway there. I'll have the crowd be quiet now; only one person will guide you. Call out to one of your friends who you want to guide you.

(The volunteer, still blindfolded and halfway down the "road," chooses a friend.)

Okay, this time only your one friend will guide you.

Ready? Go!

(Volunteer finishes walking the "road.")

You made it. Let me take the blindfold off so you can see how many eggs you stepped on!

(Take blindfold off. Usually the volunteer is pretty surprised to see peanuts instead of eggs.)

Not as messy as you thought, huh?

I have one question for you before you sit down: Which was easier, navigating when everyone was yelling at you, or when one voice that you trusted was guiding you through?

Thanks for volunteering! Let's give him/her a round of applause. Great job!

TRANSITION STATEMENT—LEADERS SAY THIS

It's pretty hard to walk by faith when we're listening to what everyone in the world is telling us what to do. Luckily we only need to listen to one voice—the voice of Jesus Christ our Lord, in whom we have put our faith.

For this session Jonathan will discuss how to put that faith into words.

Watch this!

WATCH SECTION 4 OF DVD

A quick word from Jonathan: Now you get another chance to hear what I have to say and see an example of someone sharing faith with a friend. Watch SECTION 4 of the DVD right now where we'll finally take a peek at what putting our faith into words looks like.

GROUP ACTIVITY

Your leader will take us through an activity to help us process what we just learned.

TRANSITION STATEMENT—LEADERS SAY THIS

I don't know about you, but I really enjoyed seeing an example of what it might look like to share our faith with a friend. Ashley did a pretty good job of putting her faith into words.

Could you do the same?

ELEVATOR PRESENTATION

I'll give you an opportunity to try it right now.

I need a volunteer. Who would like to try to share their faith . . . *in just 30 seconds?* Here's the deal: You just stepped into an elevator, and your friend asked you, "So what is it about you and your religion anyway?" You know that after 30 seconds, when the elevator door opens, you'll be interrupted. So you have 30 seconds to explain your faith in a real and relevant way.

Who wants to stand in front of the group and give this a shot? *(If you have a shy group, maybe talk with a couple of kids beforehand and ask them to volunteer.)*

Okay. I'm starting my stopwatch. Ready? Go!

(Give volunteer 30 seconds to present it to the group.)

Wow. That 30 seconds is pretty short, huh? Let's give our volunteer a round of applause! That was very brave.

How about another volunteer?

(Go through the exact same steps, thanking that person as well.)

LARGE GROUP QUESTIONS

1. What are the key elements we need to include when we share our faith—and if we have just a minute or two?
2. What are some elements we saw Ashley share in the video?
3. What are some verses we might want to use?

FAITH STORY ACTIVITY

In the video Jonathan reviews how this whole process works, starting with living an authentic faith, looking for open doors, and then finally asking permission to share. One way to do this is to ask your friend if you can tell him or her your faith story.

Remember, during the last session we talked about how to approach this—not being too pushy, but not being silent, either. Instead we should trust the Holy Spirit to help us look for open doors and actually walk through them. This might mean answering our friends' questions; but it could require us to bring it up. If the opportunity arises, we might find the chance to ask our friends if we can share our faith stories. This doesn't mean you use those exact words: "Can I share my faith story with you?" You might just ask, "Have I ever told you about my beliefs?" And then ask, "Is it okay if I do?"

If a friend says "yes," then you need to be prepared to share your faith story.

Jonathan mentioned that all faith stories have three elements:

1. My life without Jesus
2. Putting my trust in Jesus
3. My life with Jesus

Ashley shared her faith story and included all three of those elements. She shared that when she lived life for herself, she hurt others and felt miserable. So she put her trust in Jesus, telling him, "Forgive me. I want to put my trust in you and live totally for you." Life with Jesus wasn't perfect—bad things still happened—but now God was with her during those tough times.

That was Ashley's faith story. Each of you has a faith story. Let's practice sharing it with each other right now.

Everybody grab a partner!

Okay, choose someone to be the talker and the other to be the listener. Now when I say "Go," the talker should share his/her faith story in just three minutes. There are three elements to all faith stories, so try to take about a minute for each element. Listeners, you can help remind the talkers about the three elements if necessary:

1. My life without Jesus
2. Putting my trust in Jesus
3. My life with Jesus

Ready? Go.
(Give them three minutes.)
Okay, stop.

LARGE GROUP QUESTIONS

Now let me ask a few of you talkers:

1. How did it go?
2. What was the hardest part?
3. How did you explain step 2, putting your trust in Jesus?

Okay, now let's switch roles. The talker is now the listener and vice versa.

Ready? Go!

(Give them three minutes, then stop and ask the same three questions.)

ACTIVITY WRAP-UP

This activity gives us just a taste of what it might be like to share with our friends. Now we can see why Peter tells us in the Bible to "be prepared" to give an answer. Some of us might really need to think through how to articulate our faith into words.

Let's divide into small groups and talk about this further!

SMALL GROUP DISCUSSION QUESTIONS

Think About This: In the video, Jonathan shows us three ways how *not* to share our faith.

1. What were some of those ways?
2. Why was the PRESENTATION method so creepy?
3. What was wrong with the SCARE TACTICS method?
4. What about the example of the person who tried to WING IT? Why doesn't that work?
5. Did you come close to any of those methods when you tried to share with your partner a moment ago?
6. What could you do to be better prepared to share your faith story?

Read the following four Scriptures:

"Whoever believes in the Son has eternal life, but whoever rejects the Son will not see life, for God's wrath remains on them." (John 3:36)

"Very truly I tell you, whoever hears my word and believes him who sent me has eternal life and will not be judged but has crossed over from death to life." (John 5:24)

"Very truly I tell you, the one who believes has eternal life." (John 6:47)

However, to the one who does not work but trusts God who justifies the ungodly, their faith is credited as righteousness. (Romans 4:5)

7. What are some elements that all these verses have in common?
8. How many verses use the word *believe*? What does it mean?
9. The Romans verse uses the word *trust*. Do you think there's much of a difference between *trust* and *believe*?
10. What does the "believing" or "trusting" actually look like in your life?
11. Which of these verses might be good for you to include when explaining what it means to truly put your trust in Jesus?

SMALL GROUP WRAP-UP

We want to be ready when the Holy Spirit opens a door for us to share with our friends. One of the best ways we can be ready is to get to know Jesus better by reading his Word.

SOMETHING YOU CAN DO THIS WEEK

Let's spend some time in the Bible this week getting to know Jesus better so we can better articulate our faith.

In the video, when Ashley shares her faith story, she accurately answers several of Natalie's tough questions about belief and why Jesus saved us. Could you articulate your faith using words like Ashley does?

When we practiced our faith story with our friends, some of us might have had a little trouble explaining what "putting our trust in Jesus" actually looks like according to the Bible. Ashley presents the gospel message clearly, using examples from Scripture. The following are four facts Ashley presents that might be good to memorize. Notice that Ashley doesn't "list" these four facts; instead she makes sure that her faith story includes them.

Memorize these four facts this week, look up the Scriptures that support them, and then memorize at least one verse to correspond with each fact.

1. God loves us and wants a relationship with us. (John 3:16-17; Romans 5:8)

2. Our sin hurts us, hurts others, and messes up our relationship with God. (Romans 3:23; 6:23)

3. Only Jesus can save us from the problem of sin. (John 1:12; 14:6; Romans 3:22; 1 John 5:11-12)

4. If we want God's free gift of love and grace, we need to respond in faith, putting our trust in Jesus. (John 5:24; 6:47; Acts 3:19; Romans 4:5)

At the end of this week, get together with a Christian friend and practice telling your faith story again. This time try to include these four facts in your explanation of how someone puts his/her trust in Jesus.

FINAL THOUGHTS

Sharing your faith isn't easy. It starts with our own changed lives and then requires us to humbly and daily depend on God for strength and direction. When a door is opened, we don't want to err on the side of pushiness or silence, so it helps to listen and be a good friend while preparing to share our faith story.

A few years ago I encouraged my youth ministry leaders to undertake the same task I just asked you to undertake. I asked them to memorize those four steps, memorize four corresponding verses, and practice sharing the gospel with a Christian friend or loved one in the next week. Kevin did this and was really surprised with the result.

Growing up Kevin's family didn't go to church much. His mom went with him occasionally and always was an encouragement to him. When I gave Kevin this assignment, he decided to ask his mom if he could practice sharing the gospel with her. She was happy to help.

Kevin sat down with her that night and went through all four steps, sharing Scripture along the way. When he got to the final step, he said, "What do you think?" He was hoping to get some feedback on whether he did a good job or not. Instead, she said, "I need that."

Kevin was confused. "Need what?"

"I need to do what you said," she elaborated. "I've never done that. I've never responded like that."

Kevin was taken by surprise. "Oh . . . well okay."

That night Kevin's mom prayed and put her trust in Christ for the first time. The next Sunday she came to church with him.

I'm always amazed at the power of the gospel message when we have the opportunity to share it. Maybe that's why Paul said this in the first chapter of Romans:

> [16] For I am not ashamed of the gospel, because it is the power of God that brings salvation to everyone who believes: first to the Jew, then to the Gentile. [17] For in the gospel the righteousness of God is revealed—a righteousness that is by faith from first to last, just as it is written: "The righteous will live by faith." (Romans 1:16-17)

Take a moment and look back at your friends' names you wrote down in SESSION 2 of this book. Now . . . are you ready for real conversations about your faith?

Start Becoming a Good Samaritan Teen Edition, Participant's Guide with DVD

Six Sessions

DVD hosted by Jarrett and Jeanne Stevens

Participant's Guide by Michael R. Seaton with Jared Yaple

"What does it take for teenagers to "love your neighbor" in a global community?

Start> Becoming a Good Samaritan Teen Edition is an initiative to help teenagers live out Christ's love in world-changing ways right where they live. This groundbreaking training program helps youth groups and youth organizations explore the most pressing issues of our time—then start actually doing something about them.

Join Jarrett and Jeannie Stevens as they host six emotionally packed sessions featuring a remarkable array of global Christian leaders, including Zach Hunter, Brandon Heath, Mike Yankoski, Jason Russell, Rob Bell, Shane Claiborne, and many others.

The start> Becoming a Good Samaritan Teen Edition takes your students into the streets where, as the hands and feet of Christ, they will live out the gospel, positively impacting those suffering from poverty, social injustice, pandemic diseases, and more. Visit www.juststart.org to learn more about the nationwide church campaign experience and the growing list of national and international supporters and to access supplemental, online resources for the DVD curriculum.

Why Not Now? Leader's Guide with DVD

You Don't Have to "Grow Up" to Follow Jesus

Mark Matlock

Like most of the rest of us, Christian students tend to set the bar too low for themselves, especially when it comes to actively following Jesus. This 6-week Bible study curriculum will challenge students to accept the mission to live like Jesus now, not later, by telling the stories of adolescents from the Bible and in modern life who did—and are doing—significant and amazing things in the world and for the God who saves.

In a society where cultural adolescence is lingering into the 30s, it's no wonder Christian students often fail to confront the call to act meaningfully on their faith in Christ. It's easy to package that commitment with big ideas like picking a college, a spouse, and a career—and then to never quite get around to it. God, however, posts no minimum age on discipleship, and his book contains several examples of younger people both willing and able—in his power—to do extraordinarily difficult and necessary things with their lives for him. *Why Not Now?* will mine stories from the young lives of Miriam, Joseph, David, Solomon, Daniel, and Mary to find why and how they said yes to God before they would have been old enough to rent a car in our modern society.

Why Not Now? includes teaching outlines, commentary, group activities, discussion questions, and engaging assignments that will help students to catch the vision for imagining how much they might be capable of. Right now.

High School TalkSheets, Epic Old Testament Stories

52 Ready-to-Use Discussions

David Lynn

In just four short years, high school students develop friendships and habits that affect them for the rest of their lives. They need to be inspired through strong role models who embody Christian values. Where better to look for these influences than in the godly heroes of the Bible?

The TalkSheets series returns with another year of thought-provoking stories from the Old Testament to discuss with your youth group or bible studies. David Lynn shares discussion topics and questions written specifically with high school students in mind, promoting meaningful and thought-provoking conversations.

The stories in these pages highlight pure moral principles and practices for teenagers to learn about and emulate. Each of the 52 epic Bible stories is easy to use and fit to your lesson plan, including hints and tips to facilitate conversation. These lessons also include optional activities, giving teenagers to actively participate and have fun while they learn.

Available in stores and online!

Talk It Up!

Want free books?
First looks at the best new fiction?
Awesome exclusive merchandise?

We want to hear from you!

Give us your opinions on titles, covers, and stories.
Join the Z Street Team.

Email us at zstreetteam@zondervan.com
to sign up today!

Also—Friend us on Facebook!

www.facebook.com/goodteenreads

- Video Trailers
- Connect with your favorite authors
- Sneak peeks at new releases
- Giveaways
- Fun discussions
- And much more!